START-UP
RELIGION

THE JEWISH FAITH

Ruth Nason

Evans

Published by Evans Brothers Limited
2A Portman Mansions
Chiltern Street
London W1U 6NR

Reprinted 2007

Produced for Evans Brothers Limited by
White-Thomson Publishing Ltd,
Bridgewater Business Centre,
210 High Street,
Lewes, East Sussex BN7 2NH

Printed in China by WKT Co. Ltd.

Consultants: Jean Mead, Senior Lecturer in Religious
Education, School of Education, University of
Hertfordshire; Dr Anne Punter, Partnership Tutor,
School of Education, University of Hertfordshire.
Designer: Carole Binding

Cover: All photographs by Chris Fairclough

British Library Cataloguing in Publication Data
Nason, Ruth
   The Jewish Faith. - (Start-up religion)
   1. Judaism - Juvenile literature
   I. Title
   296

ISBN: 0 237 527669
13-digit ISBN 978 0 237 52766 2

Acknowledgements:
Special thanks to the Skillman and Wise families for their
help and involvement in the preparation of this book.

Picture Acknowledgements:
The Bridgeman Art Library (private collection): page 20
(Marc Chagall: Moses holding up the tablets before the
People of Israel, illustration from 'The Story of Exodus'
published 1966, colour litho; © ADAGP, Paris and
DACS, London 2004).
All other photographs by Chris Fairclough.

Contents

Different days

Samuel and Rebecca and their mum and dad belong to the Jewish faith.

▲ Here they are at home on a Tuesday.

belong   Jewish   faith

▼ **Here they are on a Friday evening. What is different in this picture from the one on page 4?**

לכבוד שבת

Every Friday evening Jewish people light two candles and have a special meal, with bread called hallah.
It is the beginning of the Jewish holy day called Shabbat.

candles   hallah   holy   Shabbat   5

Shabbat begins

Here is what happens in Samuel's and Rebecca's home each Friday evening.

► **Mum lights the candles.**

▼ **Everyone joins in a prayer to welcome in Shabbat.**

Can you see who is wearing a hat?

    prayer   welcome

◄ Dad **blesses** Rebecca and Samuel.

▼ He leads the family in singing a prayer to thank **God** for wine.

◄ Samuel and Rebecca break one of the **plaited** hallah loaves. They share it with the family.

blesses   **God**   **plaited**

Keeping Shabbat

Jewish people believe that God has commanded them to rest from everyday work on Shabbat.

▼ On Saturday morning many people go to a synagogue. This is a building where Jewish people worship God.

▲ Saturday afternoon is a family time.

commanded   synagogue   worship

Shabbat ends on Saturday evening. Afterwards some people have a ceremony called havdalah.

► They light a plaited candle

▼ and they smell some spices.

The smell reminds them of Shabbat.

What smells remind you of special times?

ceremony   havdalah   spices   9

What is a mezuzah?

Whenever Samuel comes out of his bedroom, he touches the mezuzah on the door frame. It is a little box, containing a tiny scroll.

mezuzah   scroll

▶ **The writing on the scroll is from the Bible. It is in Hebrew** and is called the **Shema. It says that the Jewish people should love God and keep his rules.**

◀ **People put mezuzahs on the door frames of their houses, to remind them that God is everywhere.**

Happy Hanukkah!

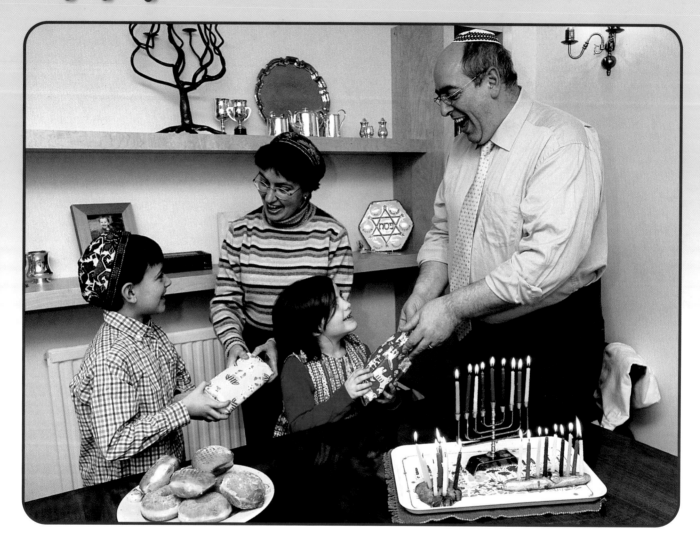

Samuel and Rebecca get presents for the festival of Hanukkah, in December. The festival lasts for eight days. Can you find out why, from the story on page 13?

festival   Hanukkah   Jerusalem

The story that people remember at Hanukkah

Long ago, in Jerusalem, the Greek rulers stopped the Jewish people from worshipping God in the Temple. Some brave Jewish soldiers fought the Greeks and won the Temple back.

◀ An oil lamp called a menorah was always kept alight in the Temple. It was a symbol of God being there. When the Jewish people won the Temple back, they found some oil to light the lamp again and a miracle happened. Although there was only enough oil for one day, the lamp stayed alight for eight days, until more oil had been made.

Temple   menorah   symbol   miracle **13**

Hanukkah celebrations

A candle-holder called a hanukiah is used at Hanukkah. It has room for eight candles, plus one called the shammas.

▲ On the first evening of Hanukkah Rebecca uses the shammas to light one candle.

▲ On the second evening, Samuel uses the shammas to light two candles.

Guess how many candles they light on the next six evenings.

hanukiah

shammas

▶ Their friends, Joshua and Ethan, are spinning a dreidel.

It has a Hebrew letter on each side. The letters stand for:

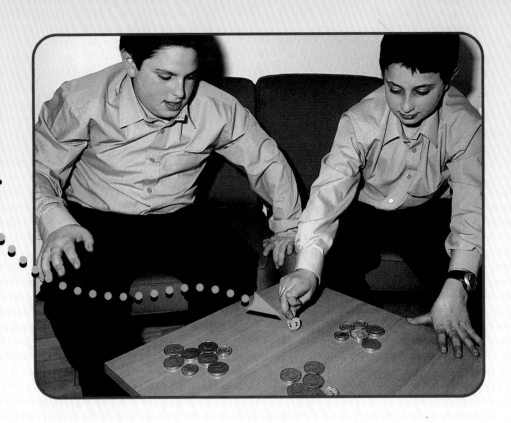

great	miracle	happened	here
נ	ג	ה	שׁ

When the dreidel stops spinning, the boys see which letter is on top. If it is ג or ה , they win chocolate coins.

▶ Which letter can you see on this dreidel?

dreidel

Passover plate

The **Passover** festival takes place in spring. There's a special plate of food on the table for the start of the festival.

Roasted egg

Parsley

Bitter **herbs,** called maror

Passover **bitter** **maror**

Roast lamb bone

▼ At Passover, people eat matzah instead of bread. What is the difference?

Haroset, made from apples, nuts and wine

These foods help people to remember an important time in the history of the Jewish people. See pages 18-19.

matzah   haroset   history   17

The story of Passover

A book called a haggadah helps people to remember the Passover story. The story begins when the Jewish people were slaves in Egypt.

 ◀ The bitter herbs on the Passover plate are a reminder of the slaves' hard life.

▶ Haroset stands for the cement they had to make for the Pharaoh, the king of Egypt.

haggadah   slaves   reminder

God told a man called Moses to say to the Pharaoh, "Let my people go". The Pharaoh said no.

God told Moses to say that, if the Pharaoh did not let the Jewish people go, God would send ten plagues to punish him. The Pharaoh still said no.

▶ Can you find out from the next part of the story what the lamb bone reminds people of?

God said the Jewish people must get ready to leave quickly. Each family must kill a lamb to eat, and put some of its blood on their door frame. That night, the tenth plague happened. All Egyptian first-born sons died, but this plague "passed over" the Jewish homes. The Pharaoh let the Jewish people go.

cement   plagues   first-born   19

Moses, a great leader

The Bible says that God chose Moses to be the leader of the Jewish people. After they left Egypt, God gave Moses rules for the Jewish people to follow.

◄ In this painting, Moses is showing God's rules to the people.

leader

Moses was worried that he would not be able to lead the people, but God said that he would help Moses. What do you think a good leader is like?

fair **strong** brave calm wise

In this book you have seen some of the rules that God gave to Moses. Jewish people still follow the rules today.

▼ **Keep Shabbat special.**

▼ **Celebrate Passover every year.**

▲ **Fix a mezuzah on the door frame.**

Further information for

Background Information

The **Jewish religion** dates back to biblical times, but is a living, diverse religion in the 'here and now'. The family in this book belongs to the Reform movement within Judaism. Care has been taken not to offend the Orthodox Jewish community, although the practices described may differ in some aspects. Try to respect this diversity, e.g. by saying 'some Jewish people ...'. Also recognize that not all Jewish people practise the religion.

Shabbat runs from Friday sunset to Saturday evening. It begins with lighting candles, representing the two commandments (Exodus 20. 8-11 and Deuteronomy 5.12-15), and a celebratory meal where two *hallah* loaves represent the two portions of manna (Exodus 16.1-26). Men and boys and some married women cover their heads as a sign of respect for God.
The 'hands in front of the eyes' gesture (page 6) is used only for the Shabbat candle-lighting blessing.
The *havdalah* ceremony says farewell to Shabbat.

Mezuzah cases contain the *Shema*, verses from Deuteronomy 6. 4-9, 11.13-21.

The **Hanukkah** story of the Maccabaean revolt is told in the first chapter of 1 Maccabees (in the Apocrypha). The *dreidel* game is said to have originated when Jewish people, forbidden to learn Hebrew, disguised their classes as a game.

The story of **Passover** is in Exodus 12.1-42. *Matzah* is eaten instead of bread. It is a reminder that the Jewish people left Egypt in a hurry; they did not have time to allow their dough to rise and it was baked into flat, unrisen *matzah*.

Familiar stories of **Moses** are his birth (Exodus 2), the burning bush (Exodus 3), the Exodus (Exodus 5-12), the crossing of the Red Sea (Exodus 14), the receiving of the ten commandments (Exodus 19 and 20).

Spelling and pronunciation: transliterations of Hebrew words may not match English pronunciation exactly. One Hebrew H is pronounced like the 'ch' in 'loch' and is written as either H or CH in English. Examples include the initial H in *hallah*, *Hanukkah* and *haroset*.

Parents and Teachers

Suggested Activities

PAGES 4-5
Talk about special meals in the children's lives.
Role-play being guests at a Friday evening meal, using candles, *hallah* loaves, grape juice.

PAGES 6-7
Talk about saying thank you, and the custom of grace before meals. Write 'thank you' cards for the cooks at school or home, with pictures of favourite food.
Tell the story of manna (Exodus 16) in role as a child at the time.

PAGES 8-9
Talk about patterns of work and rest in the children's lives.
Discuss the importance of times to rest and enjoy life.
Make contrasting pictures of weekday and weekend activities.
Make *havdalah* candles: soften wax tapers in warm water and plait them (link to science).

PAGES 10-11
Make a class list of ways to remind ourselves of things we want to remember. Focus on class rules and display them.
Write something that is important to us on stiff paper and roll it into a scroll. Making cases for these can link to D & T.

PAGES 12-13
Hanukkah can contribute to a cross-curricular topic on light.
Retell the story of the Maccabees, lighting the 8 candles of a *hanukiah* (check health and safety aspects).

PAGES 14-15
Make spinning tops with Hebrew letters (or your own alternative) and play a game where children gain or lose one or more counters or (wrapped) sweets.
Discuss the value of rules in a game and in life.

Recommended Resources

RE 'gateway' sites recommend videos, books, organizations, sources for artefacts, and other useful websites. See:

http://www.the REsite.org.uk (26 links to Jewish sites for Key Stage 1)

http://re-xs.ucsm.ac.uk (links to introductory sites on Judaism, clip art, twocandles.com etc)

http://theredirectory.org.uk

For queries and information: www.askmoses.com

Sternberg Centre for Judaism: www.refsyn.org.uk

PAGES 16-17
Discuss foods that remind children of a person or an event.
Make Passover plate collages on paper plates.

PAGES 18-19
Use a *haggadah*, a Jewish visitor or a video of a Jewish family to help you retell the Bible story.
When telling the story of the plagues, let the children dip their little finger in a glass of grape juice (for the wine representing joy) and take out one drop as you name each plague. The Jewish people remember that their rescue was at the cost of others' suffering.

PAGES 20-21
Tell some of the stories of Moses.
Draw pictures of leaders children know. Invite people with responsibilities to be interviewed. Discuss what makes a good leader.
Play a game of 'follow my leader'.

Index